To the best friend a girl could
ever hope for —

    you are always there for me,
    never judge me,
    and always support me.

I hope I give a fraction of
this back to you.

       All my love,

       Elaine

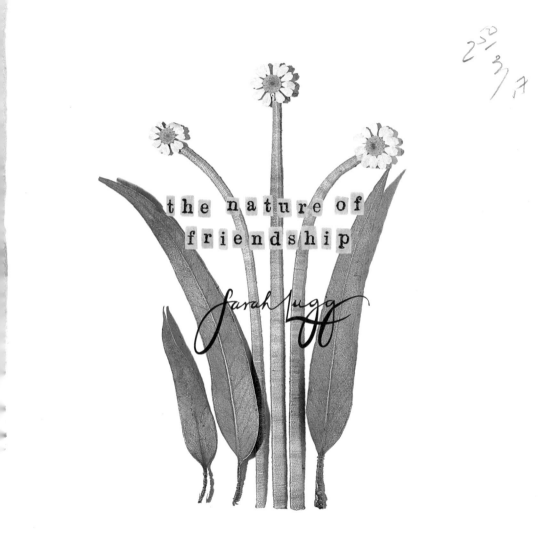

the nature of friendship

Sarah Lugg

the nature of friendship

**Andrews McMeel
Publishing**

Kansas City

www.andrewsmcmeel.com

www.sarahlugg.com

01 02 03 04 05 LPP 10 9 8 7 6 5 4 3 2 1

Library of Congress Catalog Card Number: 2001089853

ISBN: 0-7407-1972-6

Edited by Patrick Regan

Design by Stephanie R. Farley

List of Illustrations

*F*riendship is that
by which the world is most blessed
and receives the most good.

—*Jeremy Taylor*

A book of poems, *collages, and* paintings.

*F*riendship, when it is true, seems to me the most natural thing in the world. Like a growing being that must abide by the cycles of the seasons, friendship too cannot be hurried or forced into maturity. Those friendships that develop slowly, with gentle tending and generous nourishment, are those that most often stand the test of time.

As nature has provided an impetus and inspiration for my art, so have deep friendships provided inspiration and context to my life. Friendships are living things. They evolve and grow as we do, and sometimes their spirit is strong enough even to outlive us.

My friendships and my art are inextricably linked, sometimes subconsciously but often intentionally. One particular piece (actually titled "Friendship") was

inspired by my friend Margo. Visiting from America for the holidays she inquired what I would like for Christmas. I had just started to use old letters and stamps in my work, so I requested some old postcards—not everybody's ideal gift! In amongst the treasures she gave me were a bundle of old cards . . . perfect. As I set about deciphering the exquisite copperplate script, they revealed tales of friendships from the past. I proceeded to piece these snippets of friendships together and collage over them with my own thoughts and experiences on the subject.

I believe that friendship comes in many forms, and several of my most cherished ones have been fairly unconventional. When I was very young, my best friend was our beautiful and very silly Labrador dog, Honey. I was an only child and she was the best companion I could have had: reliable, faithful, soppy and always up for adventure! True friendship—at least in the eyes of a young girl.

Another lifelong friend is my godmother who has been a dear friend of my mother's since they met in school at the age of ten. I'm very lucky to have such a friend who is not only great fun and a good companion, but is also incredibly wise. This friendship amazes me all the more for the way it has evolved over the years. The bond that was forged between a grown woman and young girl— with wonderful summer outings to the beach and annual Christmas visits to a pantomime—has strengthened and stretched into a close adult friendship (albeit, still one with a wise mentor and an attentive student).

I've met best friends in the strangest of places—from a shared Jeep ride in South Africa, to less exotic locations like an exhibition hall in San Francisco. These most dear friends qualify as "soul mates" and are very rare and special indeed.

It is at the same time fortunate and frustrating to have such wonderful friends spread so widely about the globe, but the very best friend I ever had—and also the first—was always close to home. My mother and I are true kindred spirits. She passed on to me so many of her passions: gardening, cooking, decorating, and of course the arts. She also opened my eyes to the beauty of nature. She showed me how to embrace life and to share what I find. Over the course of my life, she has been the kind of friend to me that I would like to be to others.

Unfortunately, this perfect best friend passed away recently. Her passing left a tremendous hole in my life, but her presence has left me with a wealth of magical memories of our time together and the amazing inheritance of her wonderful friends.

Along with a passion for nature and for creating art that reflects its beauty,

my mother and I shared a great love for poetry. As a tribute to our immortal friendship and to all the other friendships I'm so lucky to share, I've selected some of my favourite writings on the subject of friendship to accompany my art in this collection.

I hope you enjoy these reflections on a subject so close to my heart.

However rare true love is,
true friendship is rarer.

—*La Rochefoucauld*

*T*here is no friend like an old friend,

Who has shared our morning days,

No greeting like his WELCOME,

No homage like his praise.

—*Oliver Wendell Holmes*

Of all the things which WISDOM provides
to make life entirely happy,
much the greatest is the POSSESSION of friendship.

—*Epicurus*

True happiness is of a retired nature,

and an enemy to pomp and noise;

it arises, in the first place,

from the enjoyment of one's self;

and, in the next,

from the friendship and conversation

of a few select companions.

—*Joseph Addison*

Our friendship was so assured
that we could be silent without the slightest
danger of offence.
—*Sir Arthur Helps*

moss

whispering

When to the sessions of sweet silent thought,

I summon up remembrance of things past,

I sigh the lack of many a thing I sought,

And with old woes new wail my dear time's waste:

Then can I drown an eye, unus'd to flow,

For precious friends hid in death's dateless night,

And weep afresh love's long since cancell'd woe,

And moan th'expense of many a vanished sight…

But if the while I think on thee, dear friend,

All losses are restor'd and sorrows end.

—*William Shakespeare*

Friendship never forgets.

That is the wonderful thing about it.

—*Oscar Wilde*

Friendship! mysterious cement of the soul!

Sweet'ner of life, and solder of society!

—*Robert Blair*

$\mathcal{T}$here is no wilderness like a life without friends;
friendship multiplies blessing and minimizes misfortunes;
it is a unique remedy against adversity, *and it soothes the soul.*

—*Baltasar Gracián*

Don't walk before me,

I may not follow,

Don't walk behind me,

I may not lead,

Just walk beside me and be my friend.

—Albert Camus

30

Friendship is the shadow of the evening,

which strengthens with the setting sun of life.

—Jean de La Fontaine

Sir, more than kisses, letters, mingle souls;

For, thus friends absent speak.

—John Donne

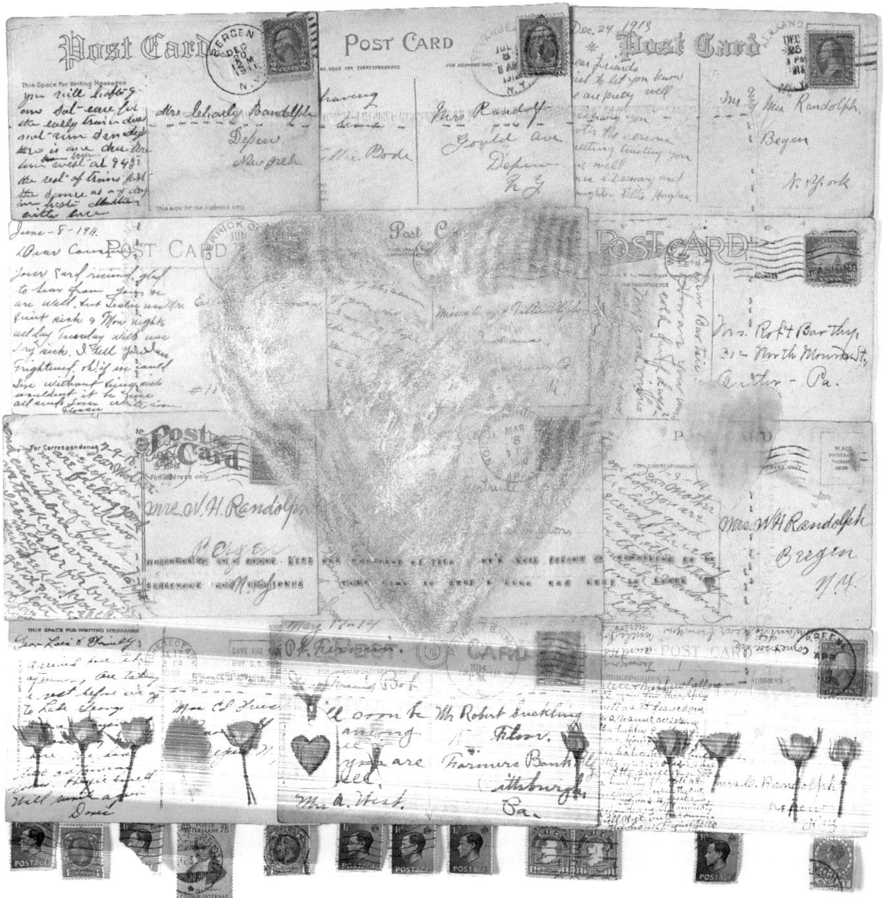

Post Card
POST CARD
Post Card
This Space for Writing Messages
This side for the Address only
Dec. 24 1913
Mr & Mrs Randolph
Bergen
N. York
June-8-1914
POST CARD
Post Card
POST CARD
Mrs. Rob't Barthy,
312 North Mountain St,
Butler - Pa.
For Correspondence
Post Card
Mrs. W. H. Randolph
Bergen
N.Y.
THIS SPACE FOR WRITING MESSAGES
May 17-14
Mr Robert Suckling
Farmers Bank Bldg
Pittsburgh
Pa.
POST CARD
POSTAGE

ove all, trust a few,

      Do wrong to none: be able for thine enemy

Rather in power than use, and keep thy friend

      Under thy own life's key: be checked for silence,

          But never taxed for speech.

                    —*William Shakespeare*

A friend is,
as it were,
a second self.

—*Cicero*

From quiet homes and first beginning,

Out to the undiscovered ends,

There's nothing worth the wear of winning,

But laughter and the love of friends.

—*Hilaire Belloc*

Go often to the house

of thy friend,

for weeds choke

the unused path.

—*Ralph Waldo Emerson*

The only reward

in virtue is virtue;

The only way to have a friend

is to be one.

—*Ralph Waldo Emerson*

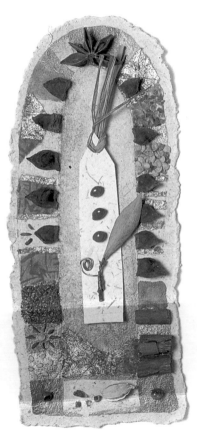

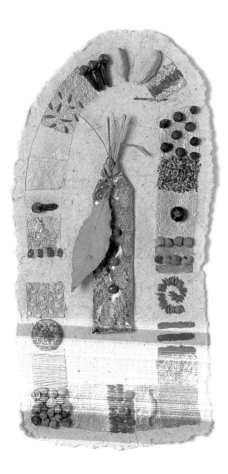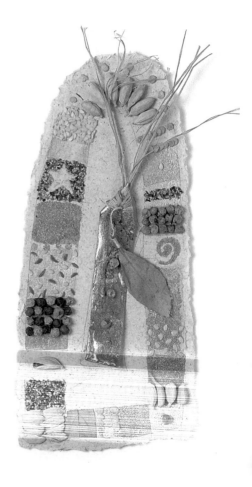

onsult your friend on all things,

especially on those which respect yourself.

His counsel may then be useful

where your own self-love

might impair your judgment.

—*Lucius Annaeus Seneca*

$\mathcal{T}$he most I can do for my friend

is simply to be his friend.

I have no wealth to bestow on him.

If he knows that I am happy in loving him,

he will want no other reward.

Is not friendship divine in this?

—*Henry David Thoreau*

The bird a nest,
The spider a web,
Man friendship.
—*William Blake*

Flowers are lovely; love is flower-like;
Friendship is a sheltering tree.
—*Samuel Taylor Coleridge*

I count myself in nothing else so happy
As in a soul remembering my good friends.

—*William Shakespeare, King Richard II*

Those friends thou hast, and their adoption tried,
Grapple them to thy soul

with hoops of steel.

—*William Shakespeare, Hamlet*

48

It is a good thing to be RICH,

and a better thing to be STRONG,

but it is a better thing to be BELOVED of many friends.

—Euripides

True friends visit us in PROSPERITY

only when invited,

but in ADVERSITY they come without invitation.

—Theophrastus

50

To lose a friend is the greatest of all evils,

but endeavour rather to rejoice that you possessed him

than to mourn his loss.

— *Lucius Annaeus Seneca*

Nothing is meritorious
but virtue and friendship,

and, indeed,

friendship is only a part of virtue.

—*Alexander Pope*

Friendship is the marriage of the soul.

—*Voltaire*

It is a sweet thing,

friendship,

a dear balm,

A happy and auspicious

bird of calm.

—*Percy Bysshe Shelly*

What through youth

gave love and roses,

Age still leaves us

friends and wine.

—*Thomas Moore*

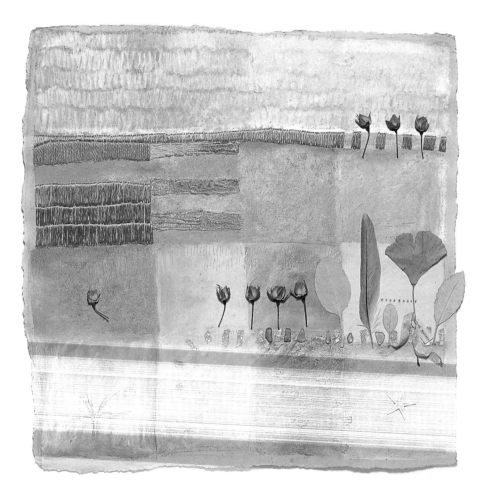

$\mathcal{O}$f all felicities the most charming
is that of a firm and gentle friendship.

It sweetens our cares,

dispels our sorrows,

and counsels us in all our extremities.

— *Lucius Annaeus Seneca*

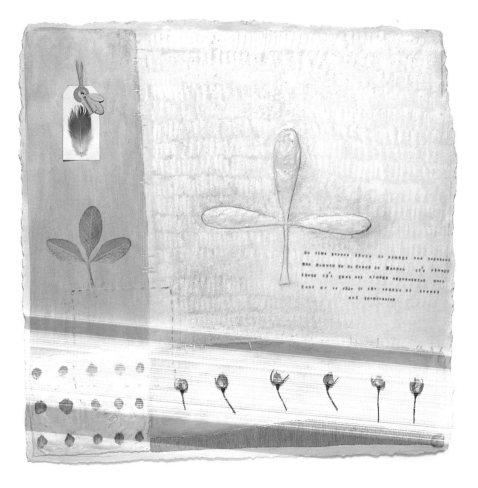

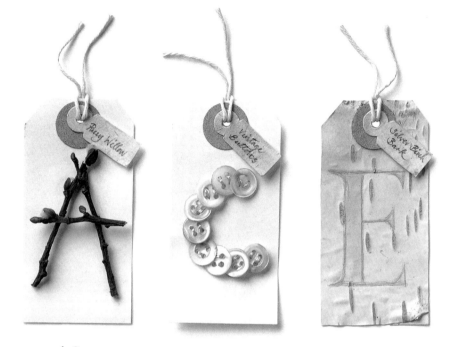

*E*ven the death of friends will inspire us as much as their lives . . .

Their memories will be encrusted over

with sublime and pleasing thoughts,

as monuments of other men are overgrown with moss;

for our friends have no place in the graveyard.

—*Henry David Thoreau*

Arise, and get thee forth, and seek

A friendship for the years to come.

—*Alfred, Lord Tennyson*

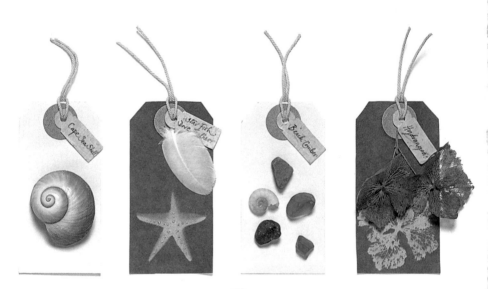

Think where man's glory
most begins and ends
And say my glory was I had such friends.
—*William Butler Yeats*